# We Live Here Too!

Kids Talk About
Good Citizenship

Written by
Nancy Loewen

Illustrated by
Omarr Wesley

Content Advisor: Lorraine O. Moore, Ph.D., Educational Psychology

Reading Advisor: Lauren A. Liang, M.A., Literacy Education, University of Minnesota

PICTURE WINDOW BOOKS
Minneapolis, Minnesota

Editor: Nadia Higgins
Designer: Thomas Emery
Page production: Picture Window Books
The illustrations in this book were prepared digitally.


Picture Window Books
5115 Excelsior Boulevard
Suite 232
Minneapolis, MN  55416
1-877-845-8392
www.picturewindowbooks.com

Printed in the United States of America.

**Library of Congress Cataloging-in-Publication Data**
Loewen, Nancy, 1964–
  We live here too! : kids talk about good citizenship / written by Nancy Loewen ;
illustrated by Omarr Wesley.
     p. cm. Includes index.
  Summary: Uses an advice-column format to define citizenship and explain how it
can be demonstrated or used in daily situations.
  ISBN 1-4048-0035-2 (Library Binding : alk. paper)
  1. Civics—Miscellanea—Juvenile literature. 2. Social ethics—Miscellanea—Juvenile
literature. [1. Citizenship.] I. Wesley, Omarr, ill. II. Title.
  JK1759 .L657 2003
  323.6'5—dc21
                                                            2002005888

To my children,
Louis and Helena—
always my best teachers

3

Hi there. This is Frank B. Wize, your friendly neighborhood advice columnist. If you haven't seen an advice column before, it works kind of like this: Your questions go into the IN pile. My answers go in the OUT pile. In between I'll be doing lots of thinking, puzzling, head scratching—and, if things really get bad, I'll ask my friends (or my parents) to help out. They've always got plenty of advice to go around.

I'm 13 years old and in the seventh grade at C. U. Fidget Middle School. My favorite subjects are lunch, recess, and gym. Science and social studies aren't too bad, either. When I grow up, I want to be a paleontologist— that's someone who studies dinosaurs—or maybe a professional skateboarder.

Lately, I've gotten lots of questions about stuff like how to help other people, what it means to be true to our country, and how we can do a better job of taking care of our planet. I've been trying to think how they all go together, and I finally got it: good citizenship! See, we all belong to lots of different groups. We live in a certain country, state, town, and neighborhood. We go to school. We might belong to a church or club. All of these groups are important, but people have to do their part to keep them working okay. That's what citizenship is all about.

Let's get to it! This is Frank B. Wize, at your service.

Hi, Frank.

There's a new boy in my class. He wears funny clothes and eats weird food. I can't even pronounce his name. My teacher asked me to show him around, but I don't want to. What if my friends think I actually LIKE him?

Robert

Dear Robert:

Well, what if you DO actually like him? It's kind of nice to have someone around who hasn't heard all your jokes. And what seems weird to you now will seem pretty normal after a while. When my friend Mikhail started coming to baseball practice, he didn't even know how to swing a bat. But now he's so good everyone wants to be on his team. (If he goes pro, I'm going to be his manager.)

A few days ago, I read something in my social studies book that blew me away. It said there are more than six BILLION people in the world. (That's a million, times a thousand, times six—and then some.) And then there are something like 6,800 languages, 267 countries, and 14 major religions. The way I figure it, that makes us ALL a little weird—to somebody.

I guess what I'm saying is, you need to chill out on this one. Maybe if you give the new kid a chance, your friends will, too. You might even end up having a lot of fun!

Frank B. Wize

Dear Frank B. Wize:

We're doing team projects in science class. Juan and Ted are on my team. They're a lot smarter than me. It's okay to let them do most of the work, isn't it?

8    Average Annie

Dear Annie:

I don't know. Is that cool with them? And do you care if you end up looking like a total slacker? How will you feel about getting a grade for something you didn't do? That's some stuff to think about.

Also, what's up with that whole "they're a lot smarter than me" routine? Are you SURE?

This reminds me of my sixth-grade art project. Cheryl, Ken, Ramona, and I were supposed to paint a rainforest mural on the cafeteria wall. Cheryl didn't say too much, and, well, we kind of ignored her. Then we started having trouble painting the monkeys. Their arms and legs looked like spaghetti. Other kids would walk by and wiggle their arms and laugh.

Finally, Cheryl said she thought she could do the monkeys. So we painted over the ones we'd done and let her try. She blasted us out of the water. Those monkeys were the best part of the mural.

So hey, Annie, who's to say you wouldn't come up with something totally brilliant? At least give yourself the chance!

Frank B. Wize

Lima Beans

Dear Frank:

My grandma's kind of strange. I eat supper with her most nights, and if I don't finish my meal, she always says, "Think of all the hungry kids in the world!" Believe me, if I could ship my meat loaf to them, I would.

Freddie

Dear Freddie:

I'd send over my meat loaf, too. Dad puts olives in it. Yuck!

About that "hungry kids" line: I've heard it tons of times. I never really got it until my family went to a talk by some people who did volunteer work in a poor country. They showed us pictures and told lots of stories. Some of the kids in those pictures looked so sad. I mean, they were hungry and sick, and there was nothing they could do about it.

I think your grandma just wants you to be thankful you've got so much to eat. I guess when you waste food, it's like you don't even appreciate it.

But here's a tip: Tell your grandma that since you don't want to waste food, maybe she should give you less in the first place. Especially on those meat loaf nights.

Hope this helps,

Frank B. Wize

Dear Frank:

Election Day is coming up, and in my class at school,
we're going to vote, too. I can't wait, but my brother
Tim says it's dumb because our votes don't count.
He's wrong and I'm right—aren't I?

Anthony

Dear Anthony:

A lot of grown-ups don't get into voting, either, even though
their votes DO count. I don't get that. It's always seemed kind
of exciting to me. The way I see it, on Election Day, the whole
country is asking for *your* opinion. And (in case you hadn't
noticed) I really like telling other people my opinions.

My teacher says it takes a lot of work to vote. First, you have
to figure out what matters to you the most. Then you have to
figure out which people would do the best job. If you want to
get it right, you have to practice. That's why I think it's
cool that you get to vote in your class. It's like you're
getting a head start.

My dad says he always feels important when he votes, like he's
just a little taller than he was before. Try telling that to
Tim. Trust me, EVERY guy likes to feel taller.

Thanks for writing. Have fun voting.

Frank B. Wize

Dear Frank:

Most of the houses on our block have flags in the window. Some people have flags on their cars, and Mrs. Johnson even planted a red, white, and blue flower garden. My family doesn't do anything like that. My neighbor Julie says that means my parents aren't good Americans. But my mom says that you don't have to hang a flag to be patriotic. Is that true? And what exactly does "patriotic" mean?

Franny in Flagstaff, Arizona

Dear Franny:

We've been talking about this a lot in my classes, so I'm ready for this one. Here's the short answer: to be patriotic means to love your country. But what the heck does THAT mean? How can you love an entire country? Well, part of it is to not space out in history class so you learn about democracy and making the Constitution and all that. Sometimes I'm blown away by stories of the super-brave people who made this country happen.

People show their patriotism in lots of ways. (Sounds like Julie doesn't get that.) Ever since the September 11 attack, people have been putting the flag up all over. And that's great. It makes people feel proud. But you don't need a flag to be patriotic. Voting and volunteering and letting the government know what you think are patriotic, too. My teacher says just keeping up with the news can be patriotic, because if we know what's going on, we'll make better decisions.

Oh, yeah, and here's another thing: Just because you love your country doesn't mean you have to hate other people's countries. A lot of people get confused about that. But if you think about it for, like, two seconds, it makes total sense. I mean, most Americans are from other countries anyway. The way I see it, America is both a place and an IDEA—a huge, awesome idea that joins us all together.

I hope this helps. You might want to ask around and see what other people think. It's a hot topic these days.

Thanks for writing,

16

Frank B. Wize

Dear Frank:

My mom says we have to get organized. She says we're all a bunch of pack rats, and she can't stand it anymore. She wants me to go through my closet and give away the toys I don't play with anymore. But what if I really need my Mighty Mangler action figure someday? And what's a pack rat, anyway?

Carlos in California

Dear Carlos:

A pack rat is someone who doesn't get rid of anything. Like my little brother, Ben. He keeps EVERYTHING—gum wrappers, movie stubs, art projects from four years ago, funny shaped rocks from the yard, little pieces from board games we don't have anymore. Personally, his weirdness doesn't bother me. Compared to him, I look pretty good.

In my experience, you've got to watch out for a parent on a cleaning kick. They don't make a lot of sense. You're going to have to be strong and make those tough decisions yourself. Otherwise, your mom will go through your stuff herself, and that could be a disaster. What I do at closet-cleaning time is, I look at each thing and give it a number: one, two, or three. One means: No way, I'm never giving this up. Two means: I like it a lot. Three means: I like it a little bit, but not *that* much. I put the things in piles, and then the "threes" are the things that get tossed. If there aren't enough threes, though, my mom and dad make me get rid of some of the "twos," too. But the "ones" are definitely safe.

It might help to think about the kids who'll be getting your things. I mean, it's not like your mom just wants to throw the toys away. That Mighty Mangler action figure will probably make some lucky kid really happy.

So if you go along with your mom, you'll be doing two good things: You'll make her happy. You'll make other kids happy. And as a bonus, it'll be easier to find things in your closet. For a little while, anyway.

Thanks for writing. Take care,

Frank B. Wize

Dear Frank:

The lady in the apartment next to ours is really old—150, at least. She hardly ever goes out. I think she's lonely. I'd like to help, but what can I do?

Philip

Dear Philip:

Hey, I think it's way cool that you want to help your neighbor lady. My friends Blake and Sydney do this thing where once a week they go visit a few old people in their neighborhood. I told them about you, and they had some great ideas. Like, when you're going to the store, maybe you could stop by and see if there's anything she needs. Or you could see if she has any chores you could help with. It's funny, but chores aren't nearly as boring at someone else's place. (And maybe your mom and dad won't make such a big deal out of YOUR chores if you're helping the neighbor lady with hers.)

Your neighbor might like to play cards or board games, or maybe you could just watch TV together. Sydney watches "Wheel o' Dollars" with Mr. Jones every Tuesday. Mr. Jones says that it's nice to have someone around, even if you're just doing ordinary stuff.

Whatever you do, though, be sure to talk to your mom and dad about it first. Parents have this thing about knowing what their kids are doing.

Hope this gives you something to go on. Good luck!

Frank B. Wize

Dear Frank:

Some friends and I have started a club. We meet behind Tom's lilac bush every day after school. But we can't agree on what our club should be about. Tom and Kelly want to draw cars, and Henrik and Isabelle want to collect bugs. Now they want me to break the tie, and I don't know what to do. Someone's going to be mad at me no matter what I do!

Rick

Dear Rick:

Wow, you really are in a tight spot. It's tough when your friends disagree. But what's funny is, sometimes disagreeing is actually a GOOD thing. It makes people try harder to find a solution.

Last year a group of us sixth graders were planning our class trip. Some kids wanted to go to Oceans o' Fun Aquarium, and others wanted to visit the bat caves out in Creepsville. Boy, did we argue. (Well, my teacher called it "debating," since we didn't throw anything or call each other names.) Eventually we came up with a new plan that worked out great. Yep, everyone had a terrific time at Timmy's Trout Farm.

I think you and your friends need to take some more time to think about what you want. There are lots of ways you could go. Maybe you could do both the car thing and the bug thing but switch days. Or you could form two clubs but have everyone get together when it's time for snacks. Or you could draw bugs and collect cars! See what I mean?

And if you pull this off and keep the club together, be sure to run for president. I bet you'll win.

Frank B. Wize

Hi, Frank!

My name is Susan, and I'm vice president of the Earth-Sea-Sky Club. I started this group with some friends because we were really worried about our planet. Did you know that a soda can or plastic milk jug can take up to 500 YEARS to fall apart and become part of the soil? Or that the average American creates 4.3 pounds of trash each DAY?

But if little things add up to big problems, then little things can add up to big solutions, too. Tell your readers we can all make a difference.

Here are some easy ways to get started:

• Turn off the lights when you leave to save electricity.

• Reuse your paper grocery bags.

• Plant trees, bushes, flowers, or vegetables.

• Walk or ride bikes instead of taking the car.

There are LOTS more things we can all do. Maybe there's an environmental club in your school or neighborhood. If not, get some friends together and start one yourself.

Thanks, Frank!

Dear Susan:

You're totally welcome, Susan. Personally, the soda can thing blows me away. I mean, do you really want your great-great-great-great-great-great-great-great-great-great-great-great-great-great-great-grandchildren picking up your trash? Not me!

Frank B. Wize

Well, everyone, thanks for checking out my column today. There's more ahead, though, so don't leave now.

# It's Quiz Time!

Be a good citizen and check out this quiz I wrote.

**1. Patriotism means:**

    A. you're a huge fan of the New England Patriots football team.
    B. you only wear red, white, and blue clothes.
    C. you care a lot about your country and its people, land, and history.

**2. You can always tell if someone's an American because they:**

    A. speak English.
    B. like baseball, hot dogs, and apple pie.
    C. know all the words to "The Star-Spangled Banner."
    D. none of the above. (You can't tell who's an American just by the outside stuff.)

**3. If you're part of a team, you should:**

    A. boss people around because YOUR way is the RIGHT way.
    B. let everyone else make the decisions, because you'll probably be wrong anyway.
    C. find a way to let everyone do their thing.

**4. When someone says, "Think of all the hungry kids in the world," they're really saying:**

    A. you should go on a crash diet.
    B. you should be glad for what you've got and not waste it.
    C. you should eat until you explode.

**5. Voting:**

    A. is a way to join with others and tell your country, state, school, or club what you think.
    B. makes you grow five inches taller.
    C. is totally B-O-R-I-N-G.

**6. Giving away things you don't use anymore:**

    A. is a form of torture.
    B. is a good way to recycle things and help other people.
    C. will turn you into a rat.

**7. Having different opinions:**

    A. should never, ever happen.
    B. means that everyone except you is 100% wrong.
    C. can actually be kind of good, because it makes you think harder about your ideas.

**8. Good citizens:**

    A. know all the state flowers.
    B. try to make the world a better place.
    C. dress in capes and tights like superheroes.

**9. Helping other people:**

    A. is an important part of good citizenship.
    B. should be done only on even-numbered days.
    C. is for someone else to do, not you.

**10. Little actions add up:**

    A. to big problems AND to big solutions.
    B. to a dance routine.
    C. to a really hard math problem.

Answer Key:

1-C, 2-D, 3-C, 4-B, 5-A, 6-B, 7-C, 8-B, 9-A, 10-A

# People I Admire

I know, I know. You'd LIKE to make a difference, but you don't know how. You're a kid. What can you do? The answer is, plenty! Here's one example:

In Ohio, a kid named Adam had a paper route. He could deliver all his newspapers in about 45 minutes, but one day, his route took six hours. He wasn't slacking off or anything—he was collecting clothes and other household things to give to this organization that helps really poor people. What he did was, he wrote a note to all his customers explaining what he wanted to do. When the big day came, his mom drove him in a truck. For six hours, they collected bags of donated stuff. A LOT of bags—something like 50 of them. Neat, huh? I bet his arms were sore after that.

You want some more examples of things kids have done? Keep reading. Maybe what they did will give you some good ideas of your own.

• An 11-year-old girl from Iowa started a program to make "care bags" for kids in need. Like, maybe the kids have gone through a hurricane or tornado or something like that, and they've lost a lot of their things. The care bags are filled with little games and books—fun stuff—and also things like soap and toothbrushes. (A toothbrush might not be the most exciting thing in the world, but I bet if you didn't have one for a while, you'd think it was the best thing in the bag.)

• In Massachusetts, kids in first and second grade started a Trash Club for their whole school. Now lots of kids are pitching in, picking up garbage so that their school stays clean. That's one way to make your custodian smile.

• Here's one that's really cool. A Florida girl raised money to get police dogs bullet-proof vests. Those vests cost tons of money, and a lot of police departments can't afford them. But this girl started collecting pennies, and got other people to collect pennies, and in two years the group raised enough money to get vests for 158 police dogs.

• Do you know what a pen pal is? It's someone you exchange letters with, even though you haven't met. In California, a boy started a pen-pal program that lets kids whose parents are seriously ill get in touch with other kids going through the same thing.

This is awesome! There are so many different ways to be a good citizen. I get all energized just thinking about it. In fact, I think I'll go out and clean up some garbage right now. Oh, wait. I've got to do the Words to Know section first. Stay with me here.

# Words to Know

Here's a list of cool words and expressions I use in the book.

**advice column—**a feature in a magazine or newspaper (or in this case, a book) where people write in with questions about their problems and some really wise (or WIZE!) person writes back and tells them what to do

**citizen—**a member of a particular country. If you're a citizen, you have the right to live in that country. You belong. You can be a citizen of other groups, too, like your state or town. And no matter where you live, you're also a citizen of the WORLD. It kind of makes you feel important, doesn't it?

**citizenship—**Okay, this is a lot like the word citizen, except that a citizen is a person, and citizenship is what people DO—all the different ways people pitch in to keep things going.

**cleaning kick—**This kind of kick doesn't have anything to do with feet. It just means that you're really into cleaning. I, myself, don't really understand how that could happen. Luckily, kicks don't last that long.

**debating—**having a polite discussion about something that people disagree on. The goal is to be so good with your words and ideas that you get others to agree with you.

**election—**an event in which people choose someone or decide something by voting. Like when you're in a group ordering pizza, and five people vote for pepperoni, and two people vote for anchovy, sauerkraut, and

tomatoes. Pepperoni wins because more people voted for it. (Whew!) That's kind of like a mini-election.

**Election Day—**the day when people in the United States choose their leaders—everyone from city council members to state governors to the president of the United States. Election Day is the first Tuesday after the first Monday in November. (Don't worry if you can't remember all that. The politicians won't let you forget.)

**government—**the people who make and apply the rules, or laws. Our lives are totally affected by the government. Ever wonder who hired the guy who plows your street after a snowstorm? Or who said it was okay to build a new baseball stadium? Or who made Thanksgiving a national holiday? Sometimes people think of the government like it's a big THING, a giant robot or something. It's really just people.

**mural—**a picture that's painted right on a wall. Murals can get pretty big. A word of advice: don't try to paint a mural at home unless you have permission. You'd be washing dishes every night for the rest of your life.

**pack rat—**a person who saves everything, even the junky stuff. But I looked it up, and guess what? Pack rats are *real* animals, too. They have big cheek pouches that they use to store food. (Just like my little brother, Ben. I've always said he looks like a rodent.)

# To Learn More

### At the Library

Lee, Milly. *Nim and the War Effort.* New York: Farrar, Straus & Giroux, 1997.

Luthringer, Chelsea. *So What Is Citizenship Anyway?* New York: Rosen Publishing, 2001.

MacDonald, Amy. *No More Nasty.* New York: Farrar, Straus & Giroux, 2001.

Miller, Elizabeth I. *Just Like Home: Como en mi Tierra.* Morton Grove, Ill.: Albert Whitman, 1999.

Pomeranc, Marion Hess. *The American Wei.* Morton Grove, Ill.: Albert Whitman, 1998.

### Fact Hound

Fact Hound offers a safe, fun way to find Web sites related to this book. All of the sites on Fact Hound have been researched by our staff.
*http://www.facthound.com*

1. Visit the Fact Hound home page.
2. Enter a search word related to this book, or type in this special code: 1404800352.
3. Click the FETCH IT button.

Your trusty Fact Hound will fetch the best sites for you!

# Index